Informing the legislative debate since 1914 _____

Forestry Assistance Programs

Katie Hoover
Analyst in Natural Resources Policy

January 7, 2014

Congressional Research Service

7-5700

www.crs.gov

RL31065

Summary

The U.S. Department of Agriculture (USDA) has numerous programs to support management of state and private forests. These programs are under the jurisdiction of the House and Senate Agriculture Committees and are often examined in the periodic legislation to reauthorize agricultural programs, commonly known as farm bills. Both the House (H.R. 2642) and Senate (S. 954) versions of the 2014 farm bill contain a forestry title with provisions affecting forestry-specific assistance programs. Both versions of the farm bill propose to repeal, reauthorize, and modify some of these programs.

Forestry-specific assistance programs (in contrast to agriculture conservation programs that include forestry activities) are primarily administered by the USDA Forest Service (FS), with permanent authorization of funding as needed. The House version of the 2014 farm bill (H.R. 2642) proposes to eliminate the permanent authorization for many of these programs. Some programs provide technical assistance—information, advice, and aid on specific projects. Other programs provide financial assistance, usually through grants (with or without matching contributions from recipients) or cost-sharing (typically though state agencies, with varying levels of contributions from recipients). Many programs provide both.

Most of the programs provide assistance to state partner agencies. The state agencies can use the assistance on state forestlands or to assist local governments or private landowners. How the states use the funds is largely at the discretion of the states, within the authorization of each program; however, the 2008 farm bill added national priorities for state assistance and state-wide assessments and strategies to focus state efforts on achieving the national priorities. Funds are appropriated for planning and implementing forestry and related land management practices—site preparation for reforestation, tree planting, thinning, pruning, fertilizing, prescribed burning, restoring watersheds, improving wildlife habitats, and other activities. Other programs provide support for protecting forestlands from wildfires, insects and diseases, and from clearing forests for non-forest uses (such as growing crops or building houses). Two programs are designed specifically to assist landowners to recover or restore forests following catastrophic events, such as wildfires. In addition, International Forestry is often included as a forestry assistance program, because it provides technical forestry help and because it has often been funded out of FS appropriations for forestry assistance programs. Finally, states are authorized to request consolidated payments, for flexibility in program administration, and several coordinating or advisory groups exist to coordinate programs or for specific purposes under one or more programs.

Overall funding for forestry assistance programs in FY2013 was $354 million. After a high of $429 million in FY2010, funding has decreased for three successive years. Funding for the forest management assistance programs—forest stewardship and urban and community forestry—has remained relatively constant over the past five years. However, funds for forest protection programs—forest health (for insect and disease identification and control), fire assistance, and forest legacy (for easements to prevent forest clearing)—are at five-year lows.

Contents

Tables

Contacts

T he federal government has numerous programs to support forest management on state and private forestlands, primarily administered by the Forest Service (FS) in the U.S. Department of Agriculture (USDA). The House and Senate Agriculture Committees often examine these programs in the periodic legislation to reauthorize agriculture programs, commonly known as farm bills. Both the House (H.R. 2642) and Senate (S. 954) versions of the 2014 farm bill contain a forestry title (as did four of the previous five enacted farm bills) and also address forests and forestry practices in several other titles. Both bills would repeal, reauthorize, and modify existing forestry assistance programs by setting authorization sunset dates and funding limits.[1]

This report describes current forestry assistance programs mostly funded and administered through the State and Private Forestry (S&PF) branch of the FS.[2] Following a brief overview, this report presents basic information on the programs to assist forestry practices, forest protection, forest recovery, and rural economies—the purposes of the programs, types of activities funded, eligibility requirements, and authorized program duration and funding level, with recent program appropriations.

Overview

Federal forestry assistance for nonfederal landowners has been a part of USDA programs for more than a century. Initial forestry assistance efforts began with the creation of the USDA Division of Forestry in 1881 (to complement forestry research begun with funding in 1876). Forestry assistance and research programs grew slowly, and in 1901 the Division was upgraded to the USDA Bureau of Forestry. In 1905, the USDA Bureau merged with the Interior Department's Division of Forestry (which administered the forest reserves, later renamed national forests) and became the USDA Forest Service (FS). Forestry assistance, the primary mission of the State and Private Forestry (S&PF) branch, together with forestry research and management of the National Forest System, comprise the three primary FS missions.

Authority for the forestry assistance programs was reestablished and coordinated in the Clarke-McNary Act of 1924.[3] This law guided these programs for more than half a century, until it was revised in the Cooperative Forestry Assistance Act of 1978 (CFAA).[4] The CFAA has been amended several times, including in the four most recent farm bills. The Food, Agriculture, Conservation, and Trade Act of 1990—the 1990 farm bill[5]—added and rewrote several of the CFAA sections. The Federal Agriculture Improvement and Reform Act of 1996—the 1996 farm bill[6]—made a few additions and modifications to the CFAA (as amended). The Farm Security and Rural Investment Act of 2002—the 2002 farm bill[7]—replaced two CFAA provisions (as

---

[1] For more information, see CRS Report R43076, *The 2013 Farm Bill: A Comparison of the Senate-Passed (S. 954) and House-Passed (H.R. 2642, H.R. 3102) Bills with Current Law.*

[2] Assistance for forestry practices is also available through many agricultural conservation programs, generally under the USDA Natural Resources Conservation Service. For information on these programs, see CRS Report R40763, *Agricultural Conservation: A Guide to Programs.*

[3] P.L. 68-270; 43 Stat. 653.

[4] P.L. 95-313; 16 U.S.C. 2101 et seq.

[5] P.L. 101-624.

[6] P.L. 104-127.

[7] P.L. 107-171.

amended) with a new provision, and created another new program. Finally, the Food, Conservation, and Energy Act of 2008—the 2008 farm bill[8]—established national priorities and a process for states to address them, while adding and modifying other programs.

There are currently more than a dozen forestry assistance programs, as shown in **Table 1**. The programs are primarily administered by the FS, with permanently authorized funding but without specified funding levels. No forestry assistance programs have mandatory spending; all require annual funding, and all are funded in the annual Interior appropriations acts. **Table 1** identifies the U.S. Code citation, the authorized duration and level of funding, and FY2013 post-sequester funding for each program. The FY2013 funding includes appropriations to the FS S&PF account and transfers from Wildland Fire Management account. Note that some programs are combined for funding purposes. Programs are listed in decreasing order of FY2013 appropriations.

Table 1. USDA Forestry Assistance Programs

Program	U.S. Code Citation	Authorization		FY2013 Funding[a]
		Duration	Funding	
Forest Health Protection	16 U.S.C. 2104	permanent	as needed	$105 million
Rural Fire Protection[b]	16 U.S.C. 2106	permanent	as needed	$91 million
Forest Legacy	16 U.S.C. 2103c	permanent	as needed	$50 million
Emergency Forest Restoration	16 U.S.C. 2201-2204	permanent	as needed	$37 million[c]
Urban Forestry	16 U.S.C. 2105	permanent	as needed	$31 million
Forest Stewardship	16 U.S.C. 2103a	permanent	as needed	$30 million
Rural Forestry Assistance	16 U.S.C. 2102	permanent	as needed	[d]
Assistance to States	16 U.S.C. 2107	permanent	as needed	[d]
International Forestry	16 U.S.C. 4501-4505	permanent	as needed	$8 million
Community Forest and Open Space Conservation	16 U.S.C. 2103d	permanent	as needed	$2 million
Emergency Reforestation	16 U.S.C. 2106a	unspecified	unspecified	$0
Community Fire Protection	16 U.S.C. 2106c	permanent	as needed[e]	$0

a. Data are derived from the detailed funding tables prepared by the House Committee on Appropriations. Data presented are the enacted FY2013 full-year continuing resolution funding, post-sequester and post-rescission, unless otherwise specified. Includes both S&PF appropriations and funds transferred from Wildland Fire Management appropriations.

b. Includes both State Fire Assistance and Volunteer Fire Assistance programs. Authorized funding is $35 million annually in cost sharing and "as needed" for other activities.

c. Includes regular appropriations—but does not include any possible sequestration effects—and additional supplemental funding provided under P.L. 113-2, the Hurricane Sandy Disaster Relief Appropriations Act.

d. Since FY1993, Congress has funded this program as part of the Forest Stewardship program.

e. Authorized at $35 million annually for FY2002-FY2007, "as needed" thereafter.

---

[8] P.L. 110-246

Many of the forestry assistance programs provide different types of aid to the states for undertaking forestry practices to improve timber productivity or to enhance other resource values. These are shown in **Table 2** as *forest management programs*.[9] For the first time since at least 1978, no *federal forestry* program exists to provide direct cost-sharing for forestry practices on private lands. However, the 2008 farm bill expanded the definition of authorized conservation practices for agricultural conservation programs generally to include forestry practices, and thus financial assistance to private forest landowners may be feasible through the conservation programs.[10]

Some programs provide assistance for protecting forestlands from wildfire, insects, diseases, and for preventing conversion of forests to non-forest uses (e.g., agriculture, residences). **Table 2** shows these as *forest protection programs*. Forest health and community fire protection activities can be applied on private lands with the cooperation of the landowner. Most other forest protection programs provide financial and/or technical assistance to government or quasi-government entities—states, local governments, communities, volunteer fire departments, and Indian tribes. The Community Forestry and Open Space Conservation program also allows grants to nonprofit organizations.

Two *forest recovery and restoration programs* provide funding directly to private landowners in response to disasters. The Emergency Reforestation Program was created in 1990, and has not been funded since 1993. The Emergency Forest Restoration Program was created in the 2008 farm bill as an amendment to an existing agricultural conservation program to assist landowners in recovering from natural disasters.

In addition, International Forestry has been included in this report, because (a) it provides technical assistance to other nations on forestry matters, and (b) it has often been funded out of S&PF appropriations.

Table 2 also shows the type of assistance available under each program. Some programs provide only technical assistance, which can range from relevant existing information to advice and aid on specific projects. Other programs provide financial assistance. Typically these programs are grants (with or without contributions from recipients) or cost-sharing (with varying levels of matching contributions from recipients), although two programs have other "financial" provisions: (1) Forest Health Protection funds FS activities to survey and to control insects or diseases on state or private lands (with the consent and cooperation of the landowner); and (2) Forest Legacy includes federal purchase of lands or easements as well as grants to states. Many programs include both technical and financial assistance.

---

[9] The forestry program to provide financial assistance to private landowners for forest management—the Forest Land Enhancement Program (that replaced the Forestry Incentives and Stewardship Incentives Programs in 2002)—was not reauthorized in the 2008 farm bill.

[10] For information on USDA conservation programs, see CRS Report R40763, *Agricultural Conservation: A Guide to Programs*, by Megan Stubbs.

Table 2. Forestry Assistance Program Activities

Program	Type of Aid	Eligible Recipients	Primary Activities
Forest Management			
Forest Stewardship	technical & financial	states	planning; tree planting; thinning; watershed restoration; wildlife habitat improvement
Rural Forestry Assistance	technical & financial	states	planning; produce & distribute tree seeds & seedlings; protect soils
Assistance to States	technical & financial	states	planning, organization, & management; data collection & management
Urban & Community Forestry	technical & financial	state & local governments, private organizations	planning; education; tree planting & maintenance
Forest Protection			
Forest Health Protection	technical & financial	governments—federal, state, & local	survey, prevent, retard, or control insects & diseases
Rural Fire Protection	technical & financial	states, volunteer fire departments	systems for fire prevention, control, & use; fire equipment & training; etc.
Forest Legacy	financial	states	purchase forestlands or easements for forests threatened with conversion to other uses
Community Fire Protection	technical & financial	communities	planning; fuel reduction; education; wood utilization & marketing
Community Forest & Open Space Conservation	financial	local governments, Indian tribes, nonprofit organizations.	purchase forestlands or easements for forests threatened with conversion to other uses
Forest Recovery & Restoration			
Emergency Reforestation	financial	private landowners	site preparation & tree planting for areas with trees killed by natural disasters
Emergency Forest Restoration	financial	private landowners	restoration of forested areas damaged by natural disasters
International Forestry	technical	other countries	planning & management; fire, insect, & disease prevention & control; rehabilitation

Assistance for Forest Management

Four forestry assistance programs provide financial and/or technical aid for planning and implementing forestry practices (establishing and managing stands of trees) on nonfederal lands. Two of the programs (Rural Assistance and Assistance to States) have been funded through a third FS program (Forest Stewardship). Historically, forestry assistance has included programs with cost-share assistance to private landowners for forestry practices on their lands, but the forestry-specific landowner assistance program created in the 2002 farm bill (the Forest Land Enhancement Program) was not reauthorized in the 2008 farm bill, and both the House and Senate versions of the 2014 farm bill propose to repeal the program.[11]

---

[11] The Forest Land Enhancement Program (FLEP) in the 2002 farm bill replaced the Forestry Incentives Program (FIP) created in the Cooperative Forestry Assistance Act of 1978 and the Stewardship Incentives Program (SIP) added in the (continued...)

Forest Stewardship

Purposes

The Forest Stewardship program was created to improve timber production and environmental protection on nonfederal forest lands. The Secretary of Agriculture, acting through the FS,[12] is authorized "to encourage the long-term stewardship of nonindustrial private forest lands." These lands are defined as "lands with existing tree cover, or suitable for growing trees, and owned by any private individual, group, association, corporation, Indian tribe, or other private legal entity."[13] Forest stewardship is not defined directly in the statute or indirectly by reference to any listing of forest stewardship practices or standards.

Section 8001 of the 2008 farm bill added a set of national priorities for Forest Stewardship of private forest conservation through federal support for state assistance. National priorities, including for allocating funding, are:

- conserving and managing working forests for multiple values and uses;

- protecting forests from threats, including "catastrophic wildfires, hurricanes, tornados, windstorms, snow or ice storms, flooding, drought, invasive species, insect or disease outbreak, or development," and restoring appropriate forest types in response to such threats; and

- enhancing public benefits from private forests, including air and water quality, soil conservation, biological diversity, carbon storage, forest products, forestry jobs, production of renewable energy, wildlife, wildlife corridors, wildlife habitat, and recreation.

Activities

The program provides technical assistance to private landowners to help them evaluate alternative actions, including:

- managing and enhancing the productivity of timber, fish and wildlife habitat, water quality, wetlands, recreational resources, and aesthetic values;

- investing in practices to protect, maintain, and enhance resources;

(...continued)

1990 farm bill. FLEP was created with $100 million in mandatory spending through FY2007, but some funds were borrowed to pay for firefighting and others were cancelled. Ultimately, only about half of the mandatory funds were actually spent on landowner assistance. FIP appropriations had been between $10 and $15 million annually through FY1994 and between $5 million and $7 million annually from FY1995 through FY2002 (except for $16.6 million in FY1999). SIP funding was more sporadic, with funds between $15 million and $20 million for FY1991 and FY1993 through FY1995, $6.5 million in FY1998, $4.5 million annually in FY1996 and FY1997, and $3.0 million in FY2002, with no funding in the other years (FY1992 and FY1999—FY2001).

[12] Throughout this report, the FS as the action agency is identified in lieu of the Secretary of Agriculture, even though the laws typically specify action by the Secretary.

[13] Typically, "nonindustrial private forest lands" exclude forest lands owned by companies engaged in manufacturing wood products, but the definition for the forest stewardship program, in 16 U.S.C. 2103a(c), seems to allow the program to be available for timber industry lands, as well.

- ensuring that afforestation, reforestation, improvement of poorly stocked stands, timber stand improvement, practices to improve seedling growth and survival, and growth enhancement practices occur where needed to enhance and sustain the long-term productivity of timber and non-timber forest resources; and

- protecting private forests from damage caused by fire, insects, disease, and damaging weather.

Eligibility

The FS provides technical and financial aid to the states, which provides information and assistance to private landowners. For states to be eligible to receive funds, they must prepare:

- a statewide assessment of forest resource conditions, including:

  —the conditions and trends of forest resources in the state;
  —threats to forest lands and resources, consistent with the national priorities;
  —any areas or regions of the state that are a priority; and
  —any multi-state areas that are a regional priority; and

- a long-term statewide forest resource strategy, including:

  —strategies for addressing the threats to forest resources identified in the assessment; and
  —a description of the resources necessary for the state forester[14] to address the statewide strategy.

The assessments and strategies are to be updated "at such times as the Secretary determines to be necessary," and are to be coordinated with the state's forest stewardship coordinating committee (see below), wildlife agency, technical committee (under Section 1261 of the Food Security Act of 1985 (16 U.S.C. 3861)), and relevant federal land management agencies.

Authorization and Appropriations

The Forest Stewardship program was added as a new Section 5 to the CFAA by Section 1215 of the 1990 farm bill. It is codified at 16 U.S.C. 2103a. Annual appropriations for Forest Stewardship were authorized at $25 million annually for FY1991-FY1995, with "such sums as may be necessary thereafter." The authorization does not expire. Funding for statewide forest resource assessments and strategies was authorized at $10 million annually for FY2008-FY2012, with up to another $10 million from other appropriations for planning under the CFAA. Annual appropriations are shown in **Table 3**.

Table 3. Appropriations for Forest Stewardship, FY2009-FY2013

(in millions)

	FY2009	FY2010	FY2011	FY2012	FY2013[a]
Forest Stewardship	$27.0	$29.4	$32.5	$28.8	$30.4

a. Post-sequester and post-rescission.

[14] For all the programs discussed in this report, the term *state forester* means the state forester or "equivalent state official."

Rural Forestry Assistance

Purposes

The Rural Forestry Assistance program was created to assist in the management and protection of nonfederal forests. The FS is authorized to assist landowners in "protecting, maintaining, enhancing, restoring, and preserving" forestlands and the values and uses they provide and in protecting forests from insects, diseases, fire, and conversion to alternative uses. The program also assists states in providing support for establishing and managing timber stands on nonfederal lands and for protecting and improving soils and water yields.

Activities

The FS is authorized to provide "financial, technical, educational, and related assistance" for "private forest land owners and managers, vendors, forest resource operators, forest resource professionals, public agencies, and individuals to enable such persons to carry out activities that are consistent with the purposes" of the program. The program may also provide "financial, technical, and related assistance" to the states to produce, distribute, and plant tree seeds and seedlings; to assist forest management practices; and to protect soil fertility and water quality and flows.

Eligibility

The FS provides assistance to state foresters for the entire program and to state extension directors for assisting forest landowners. Assistance to private landowners is through the state agencies.

Authorization and Appropriations

Rural Forestry Assistance was created in Section 3 of the CFAA, and rewritten in Section 1213 of the 1990 farm bill. It is codified at 16 U.S.C. 2102. The authorization of annual appropriations is for "such sums as may be necessary," and does not expire. Since FY1993, the program has not been funded separately, but rather has been included as part of the Forest Stewardship program. (See above.)

Financial, Technical, and Related Assistance to States

Purpose

The State Assistance program was created to foster coordination of state and federal organizations in providing assistance to private landowners. The FS is authorized to assist in developing "stronger and more efficient State organizations," to ensure that forest data are available and comparable, and to foster adoption of new technologies.

Activities

The FS is authorized to provide "financial, technical, and related assistance" to state foresters for improving organizational management and forest data collection and use. Specifically, the program is to "enable them to better fulfill their responsibilities for the protection and management on non-Federal forest lands [including] ... assistance in matters related to organizational management, program planning and management, budget and fiscal accounting services, personnel training and management, information services, and recordkeeping." The program may also be used "in the assembly, analysis, display, and reporting of State forest resources data, in the training of State forest resources planners, and in participating in natural resources planning." In addition, the FS is authorized to create "a program of technology implementation."

Eligibility

The FS provides assistance to state foresters, and for technology implementation, to "cooperators."

Authorization and Appropriations

Financial, Technical, and Related Assistance to States was established in Section 8 of the CFAA, and renumbered as Section 11 by the 1990 farm bill; it is codified at 16 U.S.C. 2107. The funding authorization is for "such sums as may be necessary," and does not expire. Since FY1993, the program has not been funded separately, but rather has been included as part of the Forest Stewardship program. (See above.)

Urban and Community Forestry Assistance

Purposes

The Urban and Community Forestry Assistance program was created to expand knowledge and awareness of the value of urban trees and to encourage the maintenance and expansion of urban tree cover. The FS is to:

- improve understanding of the benefits of preserving existing tree cover in urban areas and communities;

- encourage owners of private residences and commercial properties to maintain trees and expand forest cover on their properties;

- provide education programs and technical assistance to state and local organizations in maintaining forested lands and individual trees;

- provide assistance through competitive matching grants for urban and community forestry projects;

- implement a tree planting program to support urban open space programs, reduce carbon dioxide emissions, conserve energy, and improve air quality;

- promote demonstration projects;

- enhance the technical skills and understanding of sound tree maintenance and arboricultural practices of individuals involved with urban and community forests and trees; and

- expand existing research and educational efforts.

Activities

The FS is authorized to provide financial, technical, and related assistance to state foresters and to establish and support state information and technical assistance programs to encourage "cooperative efforts to plan urban forestry programs and to plant, protect, and maintain, and utilize wood from, trees in open spaces, greenbelts, roadside screens, parks, woodlands, curb areas, and residential developments." The FS is also authorized to cooperate directly with local governments and with interested members of the public. The Urban and Community Forestry program is directed to:

- assist urban areas and communities in inventorying their forest resources and identifying tree planting opportunities;

- assist state and local organizations in organizing and conducting urban and community forestry projects and programs;

- improve education and technical support in selecting appropriate tree species, providing for proper tree planting, maintenance, and protection, protecting individual trees, preserving open spaces, and identifying opportunities for expanding tree cover;

- assist in developing state and local tree management plans; and

- increase public understanding of the energy conservation, economic, social, environmental, and psychological values of trees and open space in urban and community environments.

In addition, the FS is to establish an "urban and community forestry challenge cost-share program" for competitive grants to eligible communities and organizations for up to 50% of project costs. State foresters make recommendations on project proposals, and the FS awards grants based on criteria developed in consultation with the National Urban and Community Forestry Advisory Council (established under Section 9(g) of the CFAA, and described below).

Eligibility

No criteria for eligibility are specified in law. Therefore, any community, private nonprofit organization, or individual has been able to apply for assistance.

Authorization and Appropriations

Urban and Community Forestry was established in Section 6 of the CFAA, and rewritten and renumbered as Section 9 in Section 1219 of the 1990 farm bill. It is codified at 16 U.S.C. 2105. The authorization of appropriations was $30 million annually for FY1991-FY1995 and "such sums as may be necessary thereafter," and does not expire. Annual appropriations are shown in **Table 4**.

Table 4. Appropriations for Urban and Community Forestry, FY2009-FY2013

(in millions)

	FY2009	FY2010	FY2011	FY2012	FY2013[a]
Urban and Community Forestry	$29.5	$30.4	$32.0	$31.3	$30.7

a. Post-sequester and post-rescission.

Assistance for Forest Protection

There are currently five authorized programs to provide financial and technical assistance for protecting nonfederal forests. Two programs are funded in multiple expanded budget line items. Forest Health and Rural Fire Protection both have two funding components, and both receive funds through S&PF appropriations and Wildland Fire Management appropriations. To date, the Community Fire Protection program has not been funded separately (though states can use Rural Fire Protection funds for the program). Lastly, the Community Forest and Open Space Conservation program was created in the 2008 farm bill. The programs are discussed below in descending order of FY2013 funding.

Forest Health Protection

Purposes

The Forest Health Protection program was created to protect trees, forests, and wood products, directly on the national forests and in cooperation with others on other lands. The FS is authorized to:

- enhance the growth and maintenance of trees and forests;

- promote the stability of forest-related industries and employment through the protection of forest resources;

- aid in forest fire prevention and control;

- conserve forest cover on watersheds, shelterbelts, and windbreaks;

- protect outdoor recreation opportunities and other forest resources; and

- extend timber supplies by protecting wood products, stored wood, and wood in use.

Activities

The FS is authorized, directly for the national forests and in cooperation with others for other lands, to:

- conduct surveys of insect infestations, disease conditions, and man-made stresses affecting trees, and to monitor changes;

- determine measures needed to prevent, retard, control, or suppress insect infestations and disease epidemics;

- plan, organize, direct, and perform those measures;

- provide information, advice, and assistance for maintaining healthy forests and coordinate use of pesticides and other toxic substances;

- develop technologies and test research results prior to full-scale application; and

- promote silvicultural and management techniques to protect or improve forest health.

Eligibility

The FS can act on its own lands. On other lands, operations "to prevent, retard, control, or suppress insects or diseases ... shall not be conducted without the consent, cooperation, and participation [including financial contributions] of the entity having ownership of or jurisdiction over the affected land." Appropriations may not be used to pay for cutting or removing dead or dying trees, unless necessary to prevent the spread of the epidemic, or to compensate for property injured, damaged, or destroyed. The Secretary may also, by contract or agreement, provide financial assistance to state foresters or private organizations to monitor forest health and protect forest lands. Finally, the Secretary, in cooperation with state foresters, may provide 50%-75% cost shares to cooperators who have established acceptable integrated pest management strategies for gypsy moths, southern pine beetles, spruce budworms, or other major insect infestations.

Authorization and Appropriations

Forest Health Protection was created as Section 5 of the CFAA, and rewritten and renumbered as Section 8 in Section 1218 of the 1990 farm bill. It is codified at 16 U.S.C. 2104. Annual appropriations are authorized at "such sums as may be necessary," except for a $10 million annual authorization for cost-sharing to cooperators on integrated pest management strategies. The funding authorization does not expire. Annual appropriations for the forest health protection program are shown in **Table 5**. The table distinguishes funds for federal lands from cooperative (nonfederal) lands, and includes funding through the Wildland Fire Management account as well as through the S&PF account. Appropriations rose substantially after the severe fire season in the summer of 2000; during the 1990s, Forest Health Protection funding averaged about $50 million annually, compared to over $100 million annually over the past five years. However, since FY2010, funding has decreased by nearly 25%.

Table 5. Appropriations for Forest Health Protection, FY2009-FY2013

(in millions)

	FY2009	FY2010	FY2011	FY2012	FY2013[a]
Federal lands	$71.4	$78.0	$77.4	$63.4	$60.1
Cooperative lands	$56.2	$60.0	$60.2	$48.3	$44.8
Total	**$127.6**	**$138.0**	**$137.6**	**$111.7**	**$104.9**

a. Post-sequester and post-rescission.

Rural Fire Protection

Purpose

Rural Fire Protection (technically, Rural Fire Prevention and Control) was created to assist in preventing and controlling wildfires, to protect human lives, crops and livestock, property and other improvements, and natural resources in rural areas. The FS is authorized to coordinate efforts and to "provide prompt and adequate assistance whenever a rural fire emergency overwhelms, or threatens to overwhelm, the firefighting capability" of states or local agencies. The program has two components, with separate funding accounts: state fire assistance and rural volunteer fire assistance.

Activities

The FS, in cooperation with state foresters, is to develop systems and methods, and assist in their implementation, for fire prevention, fire control, and prescribed fire use by state foresters, and through them, by other agencies and organizations, including rural volunteer fire departments. The FS is also authorized to provide 50% cost-share assistance "to conduct preparedness and mobilization activities, including training, equipping, and otherwise enabling State and local firefighting agencies to respond to requests for fire suppression assistance." Finally, the FS is to cooperate with the General Services Administration (GSA) to "encourage the use of excess personal property ... by State and local fire forces receiving assistance."

Eligibility

The Secretary is authorized to provide financial, technical, and related assistance to state foresters and to rural volunteer fire departments. The latter are defined as "any organized, not for profit, fire protection organization that provides service primarily to a community or city" of up to 10,000 people, "whose firefighting personnel is 80 percent or more volunteer, and that is recognized as a fire department by the laws of the State."

Authorization and Appropriations

The Rural Fire Protection program was established as Section 7 of the CFAA, and renumbered as Section 10 by the 1990 farm bill. It is codified at 16 U.S.C. 2106. Annual appropriations are authorized at "such sums as may be needed" for most activities. Up to $70 million annually, of which half is available only for state foresters and half only for rural volunteer fire departments, is reserved for cost-share assistance. The funding authorization does not expire. Annual appropriations rose steadily from $17 million in FY1996 to $24 million in FY2000, then jumped to $113 million in FY2001. Appropriations remained relatively high from FY2004 to FY2011, generally at $104 million or more annually. However, for the last two fiscal years appropriations have been below $100 million per year, as shown in **Table 6**.

Congress also continues to appropriate funds for Volunteer Fire Assistance grants. This program was authorized as the Rural Community Fire Protection program in Section 27 of the Agriculture and Consumer Protection Act of 1973.[15] This law added a new Section 816 to the Agriculture Act of 1970 (the 1970 farm bill),[16] which had amended Section 306(a) of the 1961 Consolidated Farm and Rural Development Act (the 1961 farm bill).[17] However, the program was eliminated, and replaced by an unrelated program, in Section 741(a)(4) and (5) of the 1996 farm bill.[18] Congress continued to fund the program under the Rural Housing Service in the annual Agriculture appropriations acts through FY1998. Since FY1999, the program has been funded under Cooperative Fire Protection in the S&PF branch in the annual Interior appropriations acts, under the broader authorization for Rural Fire Protection. Appropriations averaged about $2 million annually in the late 1990s, but have risen substantially since, averaging around $14 million annually in the past five years. **Table 6** shows appropriations for both state and volunteer fire

---

[15] P.L. 93-86.

[16] P.L. 91-524.

[17] P.L. 87-128, 7 U.S.C. 1926(a)(13).

[18] P.L. 104-127.

assistance programs, and includes funding through the Wildland Fire Management account as well as through the S&PF account.

Table 6. Appropriations for Rural Fire Protection, FY2009-FY2013

(in millions)

	FY2009	FY2010	FY2011	FY2012	FY2013ᵃ
State Fire Assistance	$90.0	$110.4	$97.2	$85.9	$78.4
Volunteer Fire Assistance	15.0	$16.0	$15.7	$13.0	$12.3
Total	**$105.0**	**$126.4**	**$112.9**	**$98.9**	**$90.7**

a.   Post-sequester and post-rescission.

Forest Legacy

Purposes

The Forest Legacy program was created to protect forests that might soon be cleared for non-forest uses, such as for agriculture or residences. The FS is to establish a program for "ascertaining and protecting environmentally important forest areas that are threatened by conversion to nonforest uses and ... for promoting forest land protection and other conservation opportunities. Such purposes shall also include the protection of important scenic, cultural, fish, wildlife, and recreational resources, riparian areas, and other ecological values."

Activities

The FS is authorized to "acquire from willing landowners lands and interests therein, including conservation easements and rights of public access." The FS is also authorized to provide grants to states to carry out the program.

The FS may delegate management of the lands or interests acquired "only to another governmental agency." For easements or other interests acquired, the landowner is required to manage the property "consistent with purposes for which the land was entered in the Forest Legacy Program.... Hunting, fishing, hiking, and similar recreational uses shall not be considered inconsistent with the purposes of this program." Activities may include "forest management activities, including timber management, ... insofar as the Secretary deems such activities consistent with the purposes" of the program.

Eligibility

The law establishes a three-step process for acquiring lands or easements. First, in consultation with state forest stewardship coordinating committees (established under Section 19(b) of the CFAA and described below), the FS establishes criteria for identifying eligible areas in each state, which "shall have significant environmental values or shall be threatened by present or future conversion to nonforest uses." Then, also in consultation with the state committees, the FS selects appropriate areas giving "priority to lands which can be effectively protected and managed, and which have important scenic or recreational values; riparian areas; fish and wildlife values, including threatened and endangered species; or other ecological values." Finally, private landowners with lands in eligible areas may submit applications for participation to the FS. In addition, the FS may, at the request of participating states, provide grants to the states to carry out the program.

Authorization and Appropriations

The Forest Legacy program was added as new Section 7 to the CFAA by Section 1217 of the 1990 farm bill. It is codified at 16 U.S.C. 2103c. The subsection authorizing optional state grants was added by Section 374 of the 1996 farm bill. The authorization of appropriations is for "such sums as may be necessary," and does not expire. Appropriations averaged $3 million annually for FY1996-FY1998, rose substantially, and have since declined from the peak of $76 million in FY2010, as shown in **Table 7**.

Table 7. Appropriations for Forest Legacy, FY2009-FY2013

(in millions)

	FY2009	FY2010	FY2011	FY2012	FY2013[a]
Forest Legacy	$49.4	$76.9	$52.9	$53.3	$50.5

a.   Post-sequester and post-rescission.

Community Forest and Open Space Conservation

Purpose

The Community Forest and Open Space Conservation program was established to provide financial assistance to local governments, tribes, and nonprofit organizations for preventing the conversion of forestland to non-forest uses, such as crop production or residential construction.

Activities

The FS is authorized to award grants to eligible entities to purchase fee simple title to private forestlands that (1) are threatened by conversion to non-forest uses, and (2) provide public economic, recreational, environmental, or educational benefits to communities or serve as models of effective private forest stewardship. Grant recipients must provide at least 50% of the appraised cost, and are to manage the lands consistent with the purposes of the acquisition and for public access.

Eligibility

Eligible entities apply to state foresters (or equivalent tribal officials) for grants with a description of the lands to be acquired and a plan that describes the benefits and management of the lands. State foresters submit a list of projects to the FS. The FS may allocate up to 10% of appropriated funds to state foresters for program administration.

Authorization and Appropriations

The Community Forest and Open Space Conservation program was established as new Section 7A of the CFAA in Section 8003 of the 2008 farm bill. It is codified at 16 U.S.C. 2103d. The authorization of appropriations is "such sums as are necessary," and does not expire. Annual appropriations are shown in **Table 8**.

Table 8. Appropriations for Community Forest and Open Space Conservation, FY2009-FY2013

(in millions)

	FY2009	FY2010	FY2011	FY2012	FY2013[a]
Community Forest and Open Space Conservation	$0	$0.5	$1.0	$1.9	$1.9

a. Post-sequester and post-rescission.

Community Fire Protection

Purpose

Community Fire Protection was created to assist communities in reducing threats from wildfires. The FS is to establish a program to focus federal efforts on promoting firefighting efficiency, to augment federal fire protection efforts, to expand homeowner and community outreach and education, and to establish defensible space around private homes and property.

Activities

The FS, cooperating with and implemented through state foresters, may act on nonfederal lands, with the landowner's consent, in:

- fuel hazard mitigation and prevention;
- invasive species management;
- wildfire and community protection planning;
- community and landowner education;
- market development and expansion;
- improved wood utilization; and
- special restoration projects.

Eligibility

The FS may act, through state foresters, on nonfederal lands with the landowner's consent.

Authorization and Appropriations

The Community Fire Protection program was established as Section 10A of the CFAA in Section 8003 of the 2002 farm bill. It is codified at 16 U.S.C. 2106c. Appropriations were authorized at $35 million annually for FY2002-FY2007, and "such sums as are necessary" thereafter. The authorization does not expire. To date, Congress has not appropriated funds for this program, although states can use Rural Fire Protection funds to fulfill the purposes of the program.

Assistance for Forest Recovery or Restoration

Two programs—one new and one long-standing—are authorized to provide financial assistance to landowners whose private lands have been damaged by natural disasters.[19] Neither program has provided funding for landowners in recent years—the long-standing program (the Emergency Reforestation Assistance program administered by FS) has not received any appropriations in 15 years, while the new program (Emergency Forest Restoration program administered by USDA) was created in the 2008 farm bill.

Emergency Reforestation Assistance

Purpose

The Emergency Reforestation Assistance program was created to reforest stands damaged by natural disasters. The FS can provide seedlings or reimburse some reforestation costs to eligible landowners.

Activities

The FS has the discretion to provide either tree seedlings or reimbursement of up to 65% of reforestation costs for tree stands with at least 35% mortality from wildfire; damaging weather, defined as "drought, hail, excessive moisture, freeze, tornado, hurricane, excessive wind, or any combination thereof;" or a related condition, defined as "insect infestations, disease, or other deterioration of a tree stand that is accelerated or exacerbated by damaging weather."

Eligibility

Eligible landowners include (a) persons who produce annual commercial crops from up to 500 acres of trees; (b) persons who own up to 1,000 acres of forestland; and (c) persons who own

---

[19] In addition to these two programs, a temporary Emergency Forestry Conservation Reserve Program was created to provide assistance to nonindustrial private forest landowners who experienced a loss of 35% or more in merchantable timber from the 2005 hurricanes (e.g., Hurricane Katrina). The program (as amended) provided $504.1 million from the Commodity Credit Corporation through the Farm Service Agency for 10-year contracts to establish temporary vegetative cover and to restore the land. Although the program was added to the Conservation Reserve Program (CRP; 16 U.S.C. §3831) created in the 1985 farm bill, it was exempted from the county acreage and maximum enrollment limitations of the CRP. The program was created in Section 107 of the Department of Defense, Emergency Supplemental Appropriations to Address Hurricanes in the Gulf of Mexico, and Pandemic Influenza Act, 2006 (P.L. 109-148). The 2008 farm bill (§2106(b)) renumbered the provision as Section 1231A, instead of Section 1231(k), of the 1985 farm bill.

1,000-5,000 acres of forestland, if the Secretary determines the person to be eligible. To be eligible, the landowner must not have "qualifying gross revenues" of more than $2 million; "qualifying gross revenues" generally include gross revenues from farming, ranching, and forestry operations.[20] The FS is prohibited from making payments of more than $25,000 (or equivalent value in tree seedlings) to a landowner in any fiscal year, and from providing payments to persons who receive other payments or assistance for forestry practices.

Authorization and Appropriations

Emergency reforestation assistance was established by Section 1271 of the 1990 farm bill, and is codified at 16 U.S.C. 2106a. The authorization includes no reference to funding level or expiration date. It was enacted to allow compensation to landowners who suffered substantial damage when Hurricane Hugo hit South Carolina in late 1989. Congress has not appropriated any funds for the program since FY1993; the last appropriations were for assistance related to Hurricanes Andrew and Iniki.

Emergency Forest Restoration

Purpose

The Emergency Forest Restoration program was created to assist private forestland owners "to address damage caused by a natural disaster ... on nonindustrial private forest land." The program is administered by USDA's Farm Service Agency (FSA).[21]

Activities

The FSA may provide up to 75% of the cost of emergency measures that "would restore forest health and forest-related resources." Individual or cumulative requests for financial assistance of $50,000 or less per person or legal entity, per disaster, are approved by the FSA county committee. Financial assistance requests from $50,001 to $100,000 are approved by the FSA state committee. Financial assistance over $100,000 must be approved at the FSA national office. A payment limitation of $500,000 per person or legal entity applies per disaster. Natural disasters include "wildfires, hurricanes or excessive winds, drought, ice storms or blizzards, floods, or other resource-impacting events, as determined by the Secretary."

Eligibility

Eligible recipients include owners of "nonindustrial private forest land," defined as rural land that "(A) has existing tree cover (or had tree cover immediately before the natural disaster and is suitable for growing trees); and (B) is owned by any nonindustrial private individual, group,

---

[20] Qualifying gross revenues defined at 16 U.S.C. 2106a(d)(3) as "(A) if a majority of the person's annual income is received from farming, ranching, and forestry operations, the gross revenue from the person's from farming, ranching, and forestry operations; and (B) if less than a majority of the person's annual income is received from farming, ranching, and forestry operations, the person's gross revenue from all sources."

[21] For more information, see CRS Report R42854, *Emergency Assistance for Agricultural Land Rehabilitation.*

---

association, corporation, or other private legal entity, that has definitive decision-making authority over the land."

In addition, the natural disaster must have resulted in damage that "if untreated would (i) impair or endanger the natural resources on the land; and (ii) materially affect future use of the land."

Authorization and Appropriations

The Emergency Forest Restoration program was created by Section 8203 of the 2008 farm bill, adding new Section 407 to Title IV (Emergency Conservation Program) of the Agricultural Credit Act of 1978.[22] It is codified at 16 U.S.C. 2207. Authorized funding is at "such funds as may be necessary" and does not terminate. Funding is typically provided through supplemental appropriations. Congress initially appropriated $18 million in FY2010 to remain available until expended.[23] Funds were not obligated, however, until FY2011, when final regulations were published. Annual appropriations are shown in **Table 9**.

Table 9. Appropriations for Emergency Forest Restoration, FY2009-FY2013
(in millions)

	FY2009	FY2010	FY2011	FY2012	FY2013a
Emergency Forest Restoration	$0	$18.0	$0	$28.4	$36.8

a. Includes regular appropriations—but does not include any possible sequestration effects—and additional supplemental funding provided under P.L. 113-2, the Hurricane Sandy Disaster Relief Appropriations Act.

International Forestry

Purpose

The International Forestry Program was created for the FS to provide technical assistance to other nations, especially in the tropics, on forest management for "sustainable development and global environmental stability."

Activities

The FS may provide help to other nations for conserving forests; managing forest plantations; rehabilitating damaged forestlands; preventing and controlling insects, diseases, and other damaging agents; using wood; conserving rangelands; and protecting wildlife and fish habitat. Assistance can include sharing technical and managerial skills, providing education and training opportunities, cooperating on and exchanging scientific research, and cooperating with domestic and international organizations for these purposes.

---

[22] P.L. 95-334.
[23] P.L. 111-212.

Eligibility

Assistance is provided to countries "that receive assistance from the U.S. Agency for International Development [AID] only at the request, or with the concurrence, of the Administrator" of AID. Also, the FS is directed to focus efforts "on key countries which could have a substantial impact on emissions of greenhouse gases related to global warming."

Authorization and Appropriations

The International Forestry Program was established in the International Forestry Cooperation Act of 1990, Title VI of the Foreign Operations, Export Financing, and Related Programs Appropriations Act of FY1991,[24] as amended by the Hawaii Tropical Forest Recovery Act.[25] It is codified at 16 U.S.C. 4501-4505. The authorization of appropriations is "such sums as may be necessary," and does not expire. In addition, the FS's Office of International Forestry and Institutes of Tropical Forestry were authorized in Section 2405 and Section 2407 of the 1990 farm bill, and are codified at 7 U.S.C. 6704 and Section 6706, respectively. The 1990 farm bill also directed a separate budget line for FS international cooperation and assistance. Appropriations were transferred from other FS programs for FY1992 and FY1993, then enacted at nearly $7 million for FY1994 and FY1995. For FY1996-FY2000, the FS was directed to use funds from other S&PF accounts for international programs. Since FY2001, Congress has enacted a separate appropriation for International Forestry. Annual appropriations are shown in **Table 10**.

Table 10. Appropriations for International Forestry, FY2009-FY2013

($ in millions)

	FY2009	FY2010	FY2011	FY2012	FY2013[a]
International Forestry	$8.5	$9.8	$9.5	$7.9	$7.6

a. Post-sequester and post-rescission.

Related Provisions

In addition to these several cooperative forestry assistance programs, the CFAA authorizes consolidated payments to the states (i.e., a single payment for all the programs) and establishes three groups to oversee certain programs. The 2008 farm bill replaced an existing oversight committee with a new structure and purposes. These are described below.

Consolidation of Payments

Consolidated payments are authorized in Section 9 of the CFAA, renumbered as Section 12 and amended by the 1990 farm bill, and codified at 16 U.S.C. 2108. To provide flexibility in implementing programs, states may request consolidated payments for all the authorized cooperative forestry assistance programs.

---

[24] P.L. 101-513.
[25] P.L. 102-574.

The National Urban and Community Forestry Advisory Council

The National Urban and Community Forestry Advisory Council was created under the CFAA, as rewritten in Section 1219 of the 1990 farm bill; it is codified at 16 U.S.C. 2105(g). The Council is to evaluate implementation of the national urban and community forestry action plan and to develop criteria and submit recommendations for the urban and community forestry challenge cost-share program. The Council is composed of 15 members, appointed by the Secretary, representing:

- national nonprofit forestry and conservation citizen organizations (2);

- state, county, and city or town governments (1 each);

- forest products, nursery, or related industry (1);

- urban forestry, landscape, or design consultant (1);

- academic institutions, with relevant expertise (2);

- state forestry (or equivalent) agencies (1);

- professional renewable natural resource or arboricultural society (1);

- USDA Extension Service (1);

- USDA Forest Service (1); and

- others with expertise and experience in urban and community forestry and who are not governmental officers or employees, at least one of whom is a resident of a community of fewer than 50,000 people (2).

Forest Resource Coordinating Committee

The Forest Resource Coordinating Committee was created in Section 8005 of the 2008 farm bill, replacing the USDA Coordinating Committee established in Section 19 of the CFAA; it is codified at 16 U.S.C. 2113(a). This committee is to assist in coordinating forestry assistance programs within USDA and with states and the private sector, to clarify individual agency responsibilities, and to advise on funding allocations (including competitive allocations). The Committee is chaired by the FS Chief. It is composed of:

- the Chief of the Forest Service;

- the Chief of the Natural Resources Conservation Service;

- the Director of the Farm Service Agency;

- the Director of the National Institute of Food and Agriculture;

- at least three state foresters from geographically diverse regions;

- a representative of a state fish and wildlife agency;

- an owner of nonindustrial forest land;

- a forest industry representative;

- a conservation organization representative;

- a land-grant university or college representative;

- a private forestry consultant;

- a representative from a State Technical Committee established under Section 1261 of the Food Security Act of 1985 (16 U.S.C. §3861); and

- such other persons as determined by the Secretary to be appropriate.

State Forest Stewardship Coordinating Committees

State Forest Stewardship Coordinating Committees were directed to be created by the Secretary of Agriculture, in consultation with each state forester, in Section 1222 of the 1990 farm bill, which added new Section 19 to the CFAA; the direction is codified at 16 U.S.C. 2113(b). Each state coordinating committee is to consult with other USDA and state committees on cooperative forestry programs and to make recommendations on priorities and responsibilities and on priorities for the forest legacy program. Each state coordinating committee is chaired by the state forester, and composed of federal representatives from "the Forest Service, Soil Conservation Service [Natural Resources Conservation Service], Agricultural Stabilization and Conservation Service [Farm Service Agency], and Extension Service [National Institute of Food and Agriculture]," and of others appointed by the state forester to represent:

- local government;

- consulting foresters;

- environmental organizations;

- the forest products industry;

- forest landowners;

- land trust organizations (if applicable);

- conservation organizations;

- the state's fish and wildlife agency; and

- the State Technical Committee established under Section 1261 of the Food Security Act of 1985 (16 U.S.C. §3861).

Summary and Conclusions

The U.S. Department of Agriculture—mostly through the Forest Service—administers numerous programs to support the management of state and private forestlands. Several programs provide financial and/or technical assistance through the states for planning and implementing forest management practices (e.g., tree planting, site preparation for reforestation, thinning, pruning, fertilizing, prescribed burning, and other activities) and sometimes practices to enhance other resources (e.g., restoring watersheds, improving wildlife habitat, and other activities). Some programs have been combined through the appropriations process.

Additional programs provide financial and technical support for protecting nonfederal forests from wildfire, insects, diseases, and clearing for non-forest uses. These programs cover many continuing threats to forests, although global climate change could exacerbate the effects of these threats. Furthermore, for the Forest Health program, more funds are used to protect federal lands than cooperative lands. Forest Legacy can help prevent forest clearing. The Community Fire Protection program can assist communities to prepare for wildfires, while the two emergency programs can help landowners restore forests after the disaster. These programs, as well as many of the forest management programs noted above, can help to protect and restore state and private forestlands from catastrophic wildfires and other damaging agents.

Appropriations for forestry assistance programs have fluctuated greatly since FY2000. In response to the severe wildfires in the summer of 2000, funding more than doubled from $213.3 million in FY2000 to a peak of $493.8 million the next year in FY2001. However, since FY2008, overall forestry assistance funding has averaged around $367 million, with $354 million appropriated in FY2013 post-sequester funds. Most forestry assistance programs, with the exception of the Forest Stewardship and International Forestry programs, were reduced in FY2013 appropriations for the third year in a row.

The largest sustained levels of funding have been for the forest protection programs—forest health (for insect and disease identification and control), wildfire assistance, and forest legacy (for easements to prevent forest clearing). However, funding for all of those programs has been declining since FY2010. In particular, funding for rural fire protection is 30% below FY2010 levels, despite the severe wildfire seasons of 2011 and 2012. In comparison, forest management assistance funding has remained relatively constant. Both the Forest Stewardship and Urban and Community Forestry programs have received appropriations around $30 million since FY2009.

In total, these forestry assistance programs make up less than 10% of the Forest Service's total $4.9 billion in discretionary appropriations. Overall Forest Service funding has also been declining, although at a slower rate than the decline in forestry assistance funds. However, the number, extent, and severity of wildfires continue to exceed historical levels, as does the reported incidence of forest insect and disease infestations on both federal and nonfederal forests.[26] Some may argue that both federal and nonfederal forest owners are thus facing increasing management challenges with decreasing dollars, while others may argue that decreased funding fosters innovative and cost-effective management solutions.

Author Contact Information

Katie Hoover
Analyst in Natural Resources Policy
khoover@crs.loc.gov, 7-9008

Acknowledgments

Ross Gorte, retired CRS Specialist in Natural Resources Policy, made important contributions to earlier versions of this report.

---

[26] See CRS Report R43077, *Wildfire Management: Federal Funding and Related Statistics* and USDA Forest Service, *Major Forest Insect and Disease Conditions in the United States: 011*, FS-1000, June 2012, http://www.fs.fed.us/foresthealth/publications/ConditionsReport_2011.pdf.

www.ingramcontent.com/pod-product-compliance
Lightning Source LLC
Chambersburg PA
CBHW080804290526
45790CB00008B/3583